THE BOOK

OF ME

By White Buffalo Publishing

Copyright 2021 by White Buffalo Publishing

Laura Kronske

White Buffalo Publishing

Whitebuffaloescape@outlook.com

(406) 599-5896

ISBN: 978-1-7376053-1-7

Cover design by: Kingof_designer

Formatted by: bi'tık creative

Edited by: Angelvein1

First printing

A story about the life of:

_____

_____

ABOUT THE AUTHOR

↑

Laura Kronske started White Buffalo Publishing in 2021 after she recently lost her mother suddenly, unexpectedly, and with no warning. Longing to dig up unanswered mysteries. She journeyed to uncover who her mother actually was. After many sleepless nights with no answers, Laura decided to create this book so that the next daughter to lose a mother would never struggle to find these answers like she did. She has a very large Italian family whom she is very close to and couldn't imagine any of them experiencing what she did. She only wants them to know everything about their family that they could possibly want to know. This is her way of providing that for her family and your family. Enjoy!

This book has been written for you and your family to learn, grow and understand your life together. It can be used to bring back memories through dementia, Alzheimer's, brain trauma and old age. This book can also be passed down to generations; to your, great-grandchildren so that they know who you were. I hope your children and your great-grandchildren all enjoy your life!

"Life is about the gift, not the package it comes in."

-Dennis P Costea JR.

HOW TO USE THIS BOOK

↑

"I can only Be, who I can Be"

-Laura Kronske

Imagine the joy of having your own life dictionary to reference and share with friends and families for lifetimes. Learning about yourself and being able to pass that knowledge on to your loved ones will be an amazing gift for everyone! This book will serve as a Journal of your life! The book contains approximately 365 pages, so it is possible to start one page every day and have a good start within one year. However, it will not be completed in a day or a week, but should take a whole LIFETIME to complete. Do not rush. Enjoy each entry with a laugh or a cry and note the details. What were you feeling, smelling, tasting, seeing or touching? Never think those details are unimportant; imagine describing your first trip to the river so well your ancestors could find the spot you were and live that same moment as you did. If it comes to your mind, write it down, it may be more important than you thought in the future. Go a step further and use the blank pages to collect photos, brochures, sketches and anything else that matters to you. Dive in with honesty and transparency and create your own story. This book can be passed down to your children to help them understand the family in more depth, to remember forgotten details of your life during times of dementia, memory loss, brain trauma or old age, and to reminisce when needed. Mainly though, this book will be a reference for your life lessons, important memories and moments you want to be able to relive forever. Be true to your heart and soul as you journey the pages of your book! Most of all though, enjoy your life!

"I am deeply fulfilled by all I do" -Louise Hays

This book has been written because of and dedicated to, my mother:

Cheryl (Cherie) Elizabeth Carlson Horvath

May she eternally rest in peace!

We all loved you so much!

xoxoxo

"You encouraged me to look at the past with love, acceptance and appreciation, and to the future with joy and love"

-Laura Kronske

FOREWORD

"A thousand candles can be lit from the flame of one candle, and the life of the candle will not be shortened. Happiness can be spread without diminishing yourself." -Gandhi

This is one of my favorite quotes, and my mother always spread the light; she was constantly taking care of everyone in the community. She spent her career caring for children in the school system with special needs and working with the mentally ill and elderly. She was active in her church community and volunteered in the community gardens. I rarely saw her do much for herself, but she gave so much to others. She inspires me to be the most loving, compassionate and helpful person I can be. Unfortunately, it only takes one gust of wind to blow out the candle that lit so many others.

My mother died the night before her 65th birthday. No one knows exactly what happened, but it was labeled a suicide. I always saw my mother as strong, focused and one who would never leave her children and grandchildren. But in the end, the grief and pain of life won the war, and she slipped into eternal bliss.

That was the moment my soul became lost in an abyss of grief, sorrow and confusion. I sunk into darkness and lost all of the joy and happiness that once shined so brightly through me.

This is where my journey began. I slowly regained contact with my spirituality and realized how important grief and sorrow and confusion were. It made me look very closely at every aspect of both of our lives. It made me understand that those moments were lessons that would teach me to be a stronger, more empathetic and compassionate woman. It helped me embrace gratitude for everything and everyone. I grew to realize that most of us tend to focus on the negative in our lives instead of bathing in the positive that encircles our souls.

So, I'm writing this book so that everyone can look back on their lives and appreciate every little moment and see the big picture. Life is good, and this book will prove it!

I hope for all of you to take your time completing this book, keeping in mind that someday your children will read it! God forbid it is after you pass on to the brighter light. I have allowed a page for each subject to jot down your thoughts and a blank page to include pictures, souvenirs, drawings, etc. If there is not enough space for all of your thoughts, I encourage you to write them on a piece of paper and still include it in your book. I also encourage you to date your entries for future reference and to include as much detail, photos and memoirs as possible. Hopefully, this will allow you and your descendants to smile on the beautiful soul you were instead of leaving them in a pool of tears as I was. My goal is for every family to have a never-ending encyclopedia set of the Life of their family members for all of their decedents to refer to for the rest of their lives. May the light shine brighter every day!

"You can't be brave if you've only had wonderful things happen to you."

-Mary Tyler Moore

CONTENTS

Chapter 4

Chapter 5

Chapter 9

Chapter 10

Chapter 11

"IN SCHOOL, YOU'RE GIVEN A LESSON AND
THEN YOU'RE GIVEN A TEST. IN LIFE, YOU'RE
GIVEN A TEST THAT TEACHES A LESSON"

-TOM BODETT

CHAPTER 1

"Life isn't about finding yourself; it's about creating yourself."

-George Bernard Shaw

The purest and beautiful moment in life is the day you are born! Free from any past animosity and born into the joy and happiness of your mothers embracing hug, and smile. These are the moments that will form our subconscious way of being:

MY BIRTHPLACE:

By Laura Kronske

THE TIME I WAS BORN:

_____

_____

_____

_____

_____

_____

_____

_____

_____

_____

_____

_____

_____

_____

_____

_____

_____

_____

_____

By Laura Kronske

THE BOOK OF ME

MY HOME LIFE AND SURROUNDING

I was born in:

_____

_____

_____

_____

_____

_____

_____

_____

_____

_____

_____

_____

_____

_____

_____

_____

_____

_____

BY LAURA KRONSKE

MY HOME LIFE WAS:

_____

_____

_____

_____

_____

_____

_____

_____

_____

_____

_____

_____

_____

_____

_____

_____

_____

BY LAURA KRONSKE

MY FAMILY MEMBERS:

My mother's name and birthday:

_____

_____

_____

_____

_____

_____

_____

_____

_____

_____

_____

_____

_____

_____

_____

_____

_____

_____

BY LAURA KRONSKE

MY FATHER'S NAME AND BIRTHDAY:

_____

_____

_____

_____

_____

_____

_____

_____

_____

_____

_____

_____

_____

_____

_____

_____

_____

_____

_____

By Laura Kronske

MY SIBLINGS' NAMES AND BIRTHDAYS:

_____

_____

_____

_____

_____

_____

_____

_____

_____

_____

_____

_____

_____

_____

_____

_____

_____

_____

_____

BY LAURA KRONSKE

MY GRANDPARENTS NAMES AND BIRTHDAYS:

_____

_____

_____

_____

_____

_____

_____

_____

_____

_____

_____

_____

_____

_____

_____

_____

_____

_____

_____

_____

BY LAURA KRONSKE

MY AUNT AND UNCLES' NAMES AND BIRTHDAYS:

_____

_____

_____

_____

_____

_____

_____

_____

_____

_____

_____

_____

_____

_____

_____

_____

_____

_____

_____

_____

BY LAURA KRONSKE

MY COUSINS NAMES AND BIRTHDAYS:

_____

_____

_____

_____

_____

_____

_____

_____

_____

_____

_____

_____

_____

_____

_____

_____

_____

_____

BY LAURA KRONSKE

MY FAVORITE PEOPLE: NAMES AND BIRTHDAYS:

_____

_____

_____

_____

_____

_____

_____

_____

_____

_____

_____

_____

_____

_____

BY LAURA KRONSKE

MY NATAL CHARTS

_____

_____

_____

_____

_____

_____

_____

_____

_____

_____

_____

_____

_____

_____

_____

_____

_____

_____

_____

By Laura Kronske

MY ASTROLOGICAL SUN SIGN AND MOON SIGN AND CHARTS

_____

_____

_____

_____

_____

_____

_____

_____

_____

_____

_____

_____

_____

_____

_____

_____

_____

_____

_____

_____

BY LAURA KRONSKE

MY DESTINY, LOVE, AND BIRTH CARDS

_____
_____
_____
_____
_____
_____
_____
_____
_____
_____
_____
_____
_____
_____
_____
_____
_____
_____
_____
_____
_____

By Laura Kronske

"SHOOT FOR THE MOON IF YOU FALL, YOU MIGHT CATCH A STAR"

- ANONYMOUS

CHAPTER 2

"The greater the difficulty, the greater the joy."

-Marcus Tullius Cicero

Some of us have moved around to a million different homes. Some have only lived in one their entire childhood. Either way, each home shelters us and has many hidden secrets and memories. Recall the hidden attic doors or the time you slept outside, or even the pets that may be buried in the backyard. Each home holds an entirely different memory for each soul that passes through. Try to record addresses, neighborhoods, and surrounding monuments, parks, or stores frequented.

MY HOME STORIES

By Laura Kronske

THE BOOK OF ME

THE ADDRESSES AND PICTURES OF HOMES I
HAVE LIVED IN WITH TIMETABLE:

_____

_____

_____

_____

_____

_____

_____

_____

_____

_____

_____

_____

_____

_____

_____

_____

_____

_____

By Laura Kronske

MY VACATIONS

_____

_____

_____

_____

_____

_____

_____

_____

_____

_____

_____

_____

_____

_____

_____

_____

_____

_____

_____

_____

_____

_____

By Laura Kronske

MY FAVORITE FAMILY MEMORIES

_____

_____

_____

_____

_____

_____

_____

_____

_____

_____

_____

_____

_____

_____

_____

_____

_____

_____

_____

_____

_____

BY LAURA KRONSKE

STORIES AND PICTURES OF MY BEST FRIENDS

_____

_____

_____

_____

_____

_____

_____

_____

_____

_____

_____

_____

_____

_____

_____

_____

_____

_____

_____

BY LAURA KRONSKE

PICTURES AND STORIES ABOUT ALL OF MY FRIENDS

_____

_____

_____

_____

_____

_____

_____

_____

_____

_____

_____

_____

_____

_____

_____

_____

_____

_____

_____

_____

By Laura Kronske

ALL ABOUT MY PETS, PICTURES, STORIES, AND SPECIAL MOMENTS

_____

_____

_____

_____

_____

_____

_____

_____

_____

_____

_____

_____

_____

_____

_____

_____

_____

By Laura Kronske

MY CHILDHOOD ACCOMPLISHMENTS SPORTS TROPHIES, AWARDS, AND MEMORABLE MOMENTS

My graduations from school

_____

_____

_____

_____

_____

_____

_____

_____

_____

_____

_____

_____

_____

_____

_____

_____

_____

_____

_____

BY LAURA KRONSKE

THE BOOK OF ME

KINDERGARTEN

_____

_____

_____

_____

_____

_____

_____

_____

_____

_____

_____

_____

_____

_____

_____

_____

_____

_____

BY LAURA KRONSKE

MIDDLE SCHOOL

_____

_____

_____

_____

_____

_____

_____

_____

_____

_____

_____

_____

_____

_____

_____

_____

_____

_____

BY LAURA KRONSKE

HIGH SCHOOL

_____

_____

_____

_____

_____

_____

_____

_____

_____

_____

_____

_____

_____

_____

_____

_____

_____

_____

_____

_____

_____

BY LAURA KRONSKE

COLLEGE

Extended education accomplishments

_____

_____

_____

_____

_____

_____

_____

_____

_____

_____

_____

_____

_____

_____

_____

_____

_____

_____

BY LAURA KRONSKE

"HOME IS WHERE THE HEART BEGINS."

-LAURA KRONSKE

By Laura Kronske

CHAPTER 3

*

"Learn from yesterday, live for today, hope for tomorrow. The important thing is to not stop questioning."

-Albert Einstein

My grandma Phyllis used to love to say, "families don't divide; they multiply." When I started my baby book for my first son, it was just my husband and us. Today we could barely fit all of our family members on one page. Try to dig up as many connections as possible as you dig through your family tree and genealogy.

My family trees

GREAT GRANDPARENTS

_____

_____

_____

_____

_____

_____

_____

_____

_____

_____

_____

_____

_____

_____

_____

_____

_____

_____

_____

By Laura Kronske

THEIR BROTHERS AND SISTERS AND FAMILY

_____

_____

_____

_____

_____

_____

_____

_____

_____

_____

_____

_____

_____

_____

_____

_____

_____

_____

_____

_____

BY LAURA KRONSKE

MY GRANDPARENTS

_____

_____

_____

_____

_____

_____

_____

_____

_____

_____

_____

_____

_____

_____

_____

_____

_____

_____

_____

BY LAURA KRONSKE

THEIR BROTHERS AND SISTERS AND FAMILIES

_____

_____

_____

_____

_____

_____

_____

_____

_____

_____

_____

_____

_____

_____

_____

_____

_____

_____

_____

_____

BY LAURA KRONSKE

MY PARENTS

_____

_____

_____

_____

_____

_____

_____

_____

_____

_____

_____

_____

_____

_____

_____

_____

_____

_____

_____

BY LAURA KRONSKE

.

THEIR BROTHERS' SISTERS AND FAMILIES
MY BROTHERS AND SISTERS AND FAMILIES

_____

_____

_____

_____

_____

_____

_____

_____

_____

_____

_____

_____

_____

_____

_____

_____

_____

_____

_____

_____

BY LAURA KRONSKE

MY SPOUSE AND I
OUR CHILDREN

_____

_____

_____

_____

_____

_____

_____

_____

_____

_____

_____

_____

_____

_____

_____

_____

_____

_____

BY LAURA KRONSKE

OUR GRANDKIDS AND THEIR FAMILIES

_____

_____

_____

_____

_____

_____

_____

_____

_____

_____

_____

_____

_____

_____

_____

_____

_____

_____

_____

By Laura Kronske

OUR GREAT GRANDKIDS AND THEIR FAMILIES

_____

_____

_____

_____

_____

_____

_____

_____

_____

_____

_____

_____

_____

_____

_____

_____

_____

_____

_____

_____

BY LAURA KRONSKE

MY FAMILY CRESTS

_____

_____

_____

_____

_____

_____

_____

_____

_____

_____

_____

_____

_____

_____

_____

_____

_____

_____

BY LAURA KRONSKE

THE STORIES I REMEMBERED ABOUT MY IMMEDIATE FAMILY

BY LAURA KRONSKE

MEMORIES OF MY EXTENDED FAMILY

BY LAURA KRONSKE

ALL ABOUT MY COUSINS

_____

_____

_____

_____

_____

_____

_____

_____

_____

_____

_____

_____

_____

_____

_____

_____

_____

_____

BY LAURA KRONSKE

MY PLAYMATES AND ACQUAINTANCES THAT MADE A CHANGE IN MY LIFE

_____

_____

_____

_____

_____

_____

_____

_____

_____

_____

_____

_____

_____

_____

_____

_____

_____

_____

By Laura Kronske

"YOU GET WHAT YOU GET, AND DON'T
THROW A FIT"

-KINDERGARTEN TEACHERS EVERYWHERE

CHAPTER 4

⋔

"The light in me sees the light in you"

-Namaste

The tree of life is planted from a single seed; as it grows, we branch out with different decisions and experiences. Our branches reflect our choices and soon become our children and grandchildren and important moments. Even though it seems as if branches are different, weak, strong, diseased, we are all of the same seed. We are all fed through the same root system. We are all one, even though it appears we are many. We think each branch is an individual, but we are all only one tree.

MY CIRCLE OF LOVE
THE PEOPLE CLOSEST TO MY HEART

By Laura Kronske

HOW I FELL IN LOVE AND MY FEELINGS ON IT

_____

_____

_____

_____

_____

_____

_____

_____

_____

_____

_____

_____

_____

_____

_____

_____

_____

_____

_____

BY LAURA KRONSKE

MY DATING EXPERIENCE AND SIGNIFICANT OTHERS

_____

_____

_____

_____

_____

_____

_____

_____

_____

_____

_____

_____

_____

_____

_____

_____

_____

_____

BY LAURA KRONSKE

MY NEW FAMILY

_____

_____

_____

_____

_____

_____

_____

_____

_____

_____

_____

_____

_____

_____

_____

_____

_____

_____

By Laura Kronske

MY NEW FAMILIES CREST, HERITAGE & FAMILY TREE

_____

_____

_____

_____

_____

_____

_____

_____

_____

_____

_____

_____

_____

_____

_____

_____

_____

_____

_____

_____

_____

BY LAURA KRONSKE

IMPORTANT NOTES ABOUT FAMILY MEMBERS PLACES THEY HAVE BUILT, STATUES, OR INTERESTING ACHIEVEMENTS

_____

_____

_____

_____

_____

_____

_____

_____

_____

_____

_____

_____

_____

_____

_____

_____

_____

_____

BY LAURA KRONSKE

TO MY CHILDREN:

BY LAURA KRONSKE

TO MY PARENTS:

By Laura Kronske

TO THE REST OF MY FAMILY:

_____

_____

_____

_____

_____

_____

_____

_____

_____

_____

_____

_____

_____

_____

_____

_____

_____

_____

_____

BY LAURA KRONSKE

TO MY FRIENDS:

_____

_____

_____

_____

_____

_____

_____

_____

_____

_____

_____

_____

_____

_____

_____

_____

_____

_____

_____

_____

BY LAURA KRONSKE

MY FAMILY GOALS AND MY FAVORITE ACHIEVEMENTS OUR FAMILY HAS ACCOMPLISHED.

_____

_____

_____

_____

_____

_____

_____

_____

_____

_____

_____

_____

_____

_____

_____

_____

_____

BY LAURA KRONSKE

MY CIRCLE OF LOVE, A MESSAGE OF LOVE FOR THE FUTURE

_____

_____

_____

_____

_____

_____

_____

_____

_____

_____

_____

_____

_____

_____

_____

_____

_____

_____

_____

BY LAURA KRONSKE

"AT LAST,... MY WORLD HAS COME ALIVE."

CHAPTER 5

⚜

"Do what you can, with what you have, where you are."

Theodore Roosevelt

Our lives are full of so many memories. It's hard to believe how many experiences one person can have in a lifetime. So, many that we often push many memories far into our bodies, never to be remembered again. Take your time filling out this section, let the memories pop out of your head as you recall the different periods of your life. Write in as many details as you can, and forgotten memories are bound to pop up. If you are fortunate enough to have this book your whole life, jot down all of the experiences you are having that make you happy or sad. You never know. You may look back one day and reread your stories and see things from a different, more enlightening perspective.

My favorite stories and pictures of my young life

MY FAVORITE DATES AND MEMORIES FROM PRESCHOOL

_____

_____

_____

_____

_____

_____

_____

_____

_____

_____

_____

_____

_____

_____

_____

_____

_____

_____

_____

_____

_____

_____

BY LAURA KRONSKE

MY FAVORITE DATES AND MEMORIES FROM ELEMENTARY SCHOOL

BY LAURA KRONSKE

MY FAVORITE DATES AND MEMORIES FROM MIDDLE SCHOOL

_____

_____

_____

_____

_____

_____

_____

_____

_____

_____

_____

_____

_____

_____

_____

_____

_____

_____

_____

BY LAURA KRONSKE

MY FAVORITE DATES AND MEMORIES FROM HIGH SCHOOL

_____

_____

_____

_____

_____

_____

_____

_____

_____

_____

_____

_____

_____

_____

_____

_____

_____

_____

_____

By Laura Kronske

MY FAVORITE DATES AND MEMORIES FROM COLLEGE

_____

_____

_____

_____

_____

_____

_____

_____

_____

_____

_____

_____

_____

_____

_____

_____

_____

_____

_____

BY LAURA KRONSKE

MY FAVORITE DATES AND MEMORIES FROM MY 20'S

_____

_____

_____

_____

_____

_____

_____

_____

_____

_____

_____

_____

_____

_____

_____

_____

_____

_____

_____

_____

BY LAURA KRONSKE

MY FAVORITE DATES AND MEMORIES FROM MY 30'S

_____

_____

_____

_____

_____

_____

_____

_____

_____

_____

_____

_____

_____

_____

_____

_____

_____

_____

_____

_____

_____

BY LAURA KRONSKE

MY FAVORITE DATES AND MEMORIES FROM MY 40'S

BY LAURA KRONSKE

MY FAVORITE DATES AND MEMORIES FROM MY 50'S

By Laura Kronske

MY FAVORITE DATES AND MEMORIES FROM MY 60'S

_____

_____

_____

_____

_____

_____

_____

_____

_____

_____

_____

_____

_____

_____

_____

_____

_____

_____

_____

_____

BY LAURA KRONSKE

MY FAVORITE DATES AND MEMORIES FROM MY 70'S

_____

_____

_____

_____

_____

_____

_____

_____

_____

_____

_____

_____

_____

_____

_____

_____

_____

_____

_____

_____

_____

By Laura Kronske

MY FAVORITE DATES AND MEMORIES FROM MY 80'S

_____

_____

_____

_____

_____

_____

_____

_____

_____

_____

_____

_____

_____

_____

_____

_____

_____

_____

BY LAURA KRONSKE

MY FAVORITE DATES AND MEMORIES FROM MY 90'S

_____
_____
_____
_____
_____
_____
_____
_____
_____
_____
_____
_____
_____
_____
_____
_____
_____
_____
_____
_____
_____

BY LAURA KRONSKE

MY FAVORITE DATES AND MEMORIES FROM
100 YEARS OLD AND BEYOND.

_____

_____

_____

_____

_____

_____

_____

_____

_____

_____

_____

_____

_____

_____

_____

_____

_____

_____

BY LAURA KRONSKE

"Know that to attain the sun is merely to go on seeking it"

- The things trees know

CHAPTER 6

"Strong minds discuss ideas, average minds discuss events,
and weak minds discuss people."

-Socrates

Life can change at any moment; a single idea can build a bridge to places we never dreamed of exploring. Many people could benefit from writing down all of their goals, ideas, inventions, and dreams. Keeping an invention book or a dream journal can help us to organize and express ourselves in more efficient and effective ways. Use this section to journal your accomplishments, but also future aspirations and goals. Be honest with your soul and trust your mind, all ideas can be good ideas!

MY BUSINESS IDEAS

_____

_____

_____

_____

_____

_____

_____

_____

_____

_____

_____

_____

_____

_____

_____

_____

_____

_____

_____

_____

_____

_____

BY LAURA KRONSKE

MY GOALS FOR MY CAREER

_____

_____

_____

_____

_____

_____

_____

_____

_____

_____

_____

_____

_____

_____

_____

_____

_____

_____

_____

_____

_____

BY LAURA KRONSKE

MY INVENTIONS LIST OF IDEAS THROUGHOUT THE YEARS

_____

_____

_____

_____

_____

_____

_____

_____

_____

_____

_____

_____

_____

_____

_____

_____

_____

_____

_____

BY LAURA KRONSKE

MY DREAMS FOR MY LIFE

By Laura Kronske

MY EXISTENTIAL GOALS & MY SOULS' PURPOSE

_____
_____
_____
_____
_____
_____
_____
_____
_____
_____
_____
_____
_____
_____
_____
_____
_____
_____

By Laura Kronske

MY DREAM HOUSE, AND LOCATION

_____

_____

_____

_____

_____

_____

_____

_____

_____

_____

_____

_____

_____

_____

_____

_____

_____

_____

_____

By Laura Kronske

MY ACTUAL REOCCURRING DREAMS AND WHAT THEY MEANT IN MY LIFE

_____

_____

_____

_____

_____

_____

_____

_____

_____

_____

_____

_____

_____

_____

_____

_____

_____

_____

_____

_____

By Laura Kronske

CHAPTER 7

✦

"The secret of happiness, you see, is not found in seeing more, but developing the capacity to enjoy less."

-Socrates

Attachment is that which follows identification with pleasurable experiences. Sutra s of Patanjali 11-7

Aversion is that which follows identification with painful experiences. Sutras of Patanjali 11-8

Attachment to pleasurable, or raga is another pain-bearing obstacle. We attach ourselves to pleasure because we expect happiness from it, forgetting that true happiness is always in us as the true self. When we expect joy from outside things, we become attached to those things. If we find these things make us unhappy, we create aversion toward them (dvesha).

So, both are impediments to our spiritual path. One we like because it brings us happiness, the other, we dislike because it seems to bring unhappiness. Why? Because happiness is like the musk deer. The ancient scriptures talk about this animal with a scented spot above its forehead that gives off a musk fragrance. This deer runs here and there searching for the scent, not knowing the scent comes from his own forehead. When we see a smiling face, and it makes us happy, it is because it is a reflection of our own happiness.

Write these next chapters knowing that true happiness will always reside inside you, whether or not you accomplish all of your goals.

My retirement

MY RETIREMENT GOALS AND VACATIONS

By Laura Kronske

MY MUST DO BEFORE I DIE.
TO DO LIST

_____

_____

_____

_____

_____

_____

_____

_____

_____

_____

_____

_____

_____

_____

_____

_____

_____

_____

_____

BY LAURA KRONSKE

By Laura Kronske

CHAPTER 8

✦

"You can't have everything... where would you put it?"

-Steven's wright

I have seen many elders of my family pass on to the next life in peace. However, after death when it is time to bequeath possessions, it seems to get awkward and even cruel. My Mother and her sisters stopped talking after arguing over diamonds and fur coats of my grandmas when she died. I have seen possessions sprawled out on tables for the taking, but no one even wanted them, because they had no idea the history and memories that they held. I walked into my own mother's house and found a garage full of her special belongings ready to be hauled off to goodwill, without any of her children knowing it was set to be donated. Thank God I was able to walk in at the right time and gather what I could. Then my other grandma passed away, but she was ready! On her 80th birthday we threw her a huge party, she had developed colon cancer and knew she was passing soon. When the entire family was there, she pulled out a list of all of her possessions and passed it around first to her children and grandchildren and then to her close friends. We all put our name next to a few items that were important to us and really reminded us of her. When she passed her daughter distributed it all accordingly. It was the first time I wasn't disgusted at how the family members handled possessions after death. I encourage you to do the same, however, I encourage you to take it a step forward and include the personal and family history of each item. Eventually, we forget the stories but writing them down will help preserve the memories they are passed down through the generations!

My personal item stories

HISTORY OF JEWELRY, FURNITURE AND ANTIQUES
THAT WILL BE PASSED DOWN AT DEATH

By Laura Kronske

LIST OF THE POSSESSIONS I WILL HAVE AT DEATH AND A PLACE TO WRITE WHO WILL GET THEM (A LIST TO SIGN UP FOR WHAT THEY WANT FROM ME WHEN I DIE).

_____

_____

_____

_____

_____

_____

_____

_____

_____

_____

_____

_____

_____

_____

_____

_____

_____

_____

BY LAURA KRONSKE

"A TRULY HAPPY PERSON IS ONE WHO CAN ENJOY THE SCENERY WHILE ON A DETOUR"

-ANONYMOUS

CHAPTER 9

⋏

"Turn your face to the sun and the shadows
will fall behind you."

-Maori proverb

Think of our mind like a radio, constantly sending out signals to the universe to guide your life. You can wish for anything you want, and as long as you believe it, you will get it. When we open our minds to this possibility, we can magnify our achievements and happiness tenfold. Everything you have achieved in life is a result of you going out and getting it. Inspirational quotes, stories, and inspiring family members and friends help us to stay focused on the positive when we feel down or unable to remain strong. Record these messages to help the next generation remain positive and secure!

Life is Great!

MY LIFE IS GOOD FAVORITE PICTURES AND MEMORIES TO BE PASSED DOWN FROM GENERATION TO GENERATION

_____

_____

_____

_____

_____

_____

_____

_____

_____

_____

_____

_____

_____

_____

_____

_____

_____

_____

_____

_____

By Laura Kronske

MY FAVORITE INSPIRATIONAL QUOTE

_____

_____

_____

_____

_____

_____

_____

_____

_____

_____

_____

_____

_____

_____

_____

_____

_____

BY LAURA KRONSKE

MY FAVORITE INSPIRATIONAL STORIES

_____

_____

_____

_____

_____

_____

_____

_____

_____

_____

_____

_____

_____

_____

_____

_____

_____

_____

_____

BY LAURA KRONSKE

MY FAVORITE INSPIRATIONAL PICTURES

BY LAURA KRONSKE

MY MESSAGE TO MY FAMILY

_____

_____

_____

_____

_____

_____

_____

_____

_____

_____

_____

_____

_____

_____

_____

_____

_____

_____

_____

_____

BY LAURA KRONSKE

WORDS TO REMEMBER ME BY

_____

_____

_____

_____

_____

_____

_____

_____

_____

_____

_____

_____

_____

_____

_____

_____

_____

_____

_____

BY LAURA KRONSKE

"THE ONLY CONSTANT IS CHANGE"

- TAOISM

CHAPTER 10

"The score never interested me, only the game."

-Mae west

We are taught that if we are hurt or sick, to go to traditional doctors. We are scorned and called names for trying other healing modalities. The truth is the traditional doctor has only been around for a few hundred years. Other healing modalities have been utilized for thousands and thousands of years. It does not cause harm to anyone to explore the different options you have when healing yourself. Looking at metaphysical reasons for pain, past life trauma repercussions, the way the stars were aligned at your birth, and the ailments in our body all help us understand the whole picture of our abilities and disabilities. Looking at the different healing options as separate pieces of a pie helps us understand that we cannot see the benefits of the other without one. Putting all of our information together in one spot can only be helpful.

All of my secrets

MY SECRET TIPS TO LIFE

BY LAURA KRONSKE

MY BEST RECIPES

_____

_____

_____

_____

_____

_____

_____

_____

_____

_____

_____

_____

_____

_____

_____

_____

_____

_____

_____

_____

_____

BY LAURA KRONSKE

MY HOROSCOPE READINGS

_____

_____

_____

_____

_____

_____

_____

_____

_____

_____

_____

_____

_____

_____

_____

_____

_____

_____

_____

_____

_____

BY LAURA KRONSKE

MY BIRTHDAY CARD INTERPRETATION

BY LAURA KRONSKE

MY VIEW OF HOLISTIC READINGS

BY LAURA KRONSKE

MY NUMEROLOGY CHARTS

BY LAURA KRONSKE

MY AYURVEDIC DOSHA AND SUGGESTIONS

BY LAURA KRONSKE

MY TAROT CARD READINGS AND WHAT I GATHERED FROM THEM

_____

_____

_____

_____

_____

_____

_____

_____

_____

_____

_____

_____

_____

_____

_____

_____

_____

_____

_____

BY LAURA KRONSKE

MY PSYCHIC READINGS AND MY THOUGHTS

BY LAURA KRONSKE

MY YOGA FLOWS AND WHAT THEY DO FOR ME

_____
_____
_____
_____
_____
_____
_____
_____
_____
_____
_____
_____
_____
_____
_____
_____
_____
_____

BY LAURA KRONSKE

MY SPIRIT ANIMAL

BY LAURA KRONSKE

MY ARCHANGEL

_____

_____

_____

_____

_____

_____

_____

_____

_____

_____

_____

_____

_____

_____

_____

_____

_____

_____

_____

_____

BY LAURA KRONSKE

MY FINGERPRINTS, DRAWING OF BOTH PALMS AND PALM READING

By Laura Kronske

THE BOOK OF ME

MY DESTINY CARD IMPORTANT MOMENTS

_____

_____

_____

_____

_____

_____

_____

_____

_____

_____

_____

_____

_____

_____

_____

_____

_____

_____

_____

_____

_____

_____

BY LAURA KRONSKE

MY LOVE CARD AND INTERPRETATION

_____

_____

_____

_____

_____

_____

_____

_____

_____

_____

_____

_____

_____

_____

_____

_____

_____

_____

_____

_____

_____

BY LAURA KRONSKE

WHAT MY AURA LOOKS LIKE

BY LAURA KRONSKE

MY CHAKRA CHALLENGES AND STRENGTHS

BY LAURA KRONSKE

MY PAST LIVE READINGS AND THOUGHTS

_____

_____

_____

_____

_____

_____

_____

_____

_____

_____

_____

_____

_____

_____

_____

_____

_____

_____

_____

_____

BY LAURA KRONSKE

MY PERSONAL CHALLENGES AND HOW I OVERCAME THEM, AND THE LESSONS THEY TAUGHT ME

BY LAURA KRONSKE

MY WORDS OF WISDOM

_____

_____

_____

_____

_____

_____

_____

_____

_____

_____

_____

_____

_____

_____

_____

_____

_____

_____

_____

_____

_____

_____

BY LAURA KRONSKE

"HOW DO YOU HOLISTICALLY HEAL THE
WORLD WITHOUT DEPLETING IT? YOU
SUSTAIN IT, REDUCE, RENEW, RELIVE"

-LAURA KRONSKE

CHAPTER 11

🔱

"Who am I?"

-Rig Veda

Sometimes it's a life-changing moment that shapes our personality, sometimes it's the little things. There is so much we get to experience throughout life it really is impossible to capture it all. However, I would love for you to try! Here are some less meaningful but actually very meaningful topics I encourage you to explore. Someday your loved ones may look to this book for guidance on random situations. I hope you and they are able to find all that is needed.

Fun Facts and memories

PRESIDENTS AND LEADERS THROUGHOUT MY LIFE

BY LAURA KRONSKE

WARS I LIVED THROUGH

BY LAURA KRONSKE

FAVORITE HOLIDAYS

BY LAURA KRONSKE

FAVORITE VACATIONS

BY LAURA KRONSKE

FAVORITE PLACES TO TRAVEL

_____

_____

_____

_____

_____

_____

_____

_____

_____

_____

_____

_____

_____

_____

_____

_____

_____

_____

By Laura Kronske

FAVORITE FOODS AND ALLERGIES

_____

_____

_____

_____

_____

_____

_____

_____

_____

_____

_____

_____

_____

_____

_____

_____

_____

_____

_____

BY LAURA KRONSKE

DISAPPOINTMENTS AND BLESSINGS

BY LAURA KRONSKE

TEACHERS I REMEMBER

_____

_____

_____

_____

_____

_____

_____

_____

_____

_____

_____

_____

_____

_____

_____

_____

_____

_____

_____

_____

_____

BY LAURA KRONSKE

GIFTS I REMEMBER

_____

_____

_____

_____

_____

_____

_____

_____

_____

_____

_____

_____

_____

_____

_____

_____

_____

_____

_____

BY LAURA KRONSKE

LIFE LESSONS LEARNED

BY LAURA KRONSKE

MOMENTS THAT AFFECTED MY LIFE

By Laura Kronske

MIDLIFE CRISES

_____

_____

_____

_____

_____

_____

_____

_____

_____

_____

_____

_____

_____

_____

_____

_____

_____

_____

_____

_____

_____

BY LAURA KRONSKE

COPING SKILLS I HAVE LEARNED

_____
_____
_____
_____
_____
_____
_____
_____
_____
_____
_____
_____
_____
_____
_____
_____
_____
_____
_____
_____
_____

BY LAURA KRONSKE

CARS I REMEMBER

_____

_____

_____

_____

_____

_____

_____

_____

_____

_____

_____

_____

_____

_____

_____

_____

_____

_____

_____

_____

BY LAURA KRONSKE

FAVORITE MUSIC AND SONGS

By Laura Kronske

FAVORITE BOOKS AND AUTHORS

By Laura Kronske

MY RESUME

_____

_____

_____

_____

_____

_____

_____

_____

_____

_____

_____

_____

_____

_____

_____

_____

_____

_____

_____

_____

By Laura Kronske

STORIES OUR CHILDREN SHOULD REMEMBER

_____

_____

_____

_____

_____

_____

_____

_____

_____

_____

_____

_____

_____

_____

_____

_____

_____

_____

_____

_____

_____

_____

By Laura Kronske

GARDENING AND PLANTING TIPS

_____

_____

_____

_____

_____

_____

_____

_____

_____

_____

_____

_____

_____

_____

_____

_____

_____

_____

_____

_____

_____

_____

_____

_____

By Laura Kronske

MOON PHASES AND WHAT THEY REPRESENT TO YOU

_____

_____

_____

_____

_____

_____

_____

_____

_____

_____

_____

_____

_____

_____

_____

_____

_____

_____

_____

_____

_____

_____

BY LAURA KRONSKE

.

MEDICINAL RECIPES TO REMEMBER

_____

_____

_____

_____

_____

_____

_____

_____

_____

_____

_____

_____

_____

_____

_____

_____

_____

_____

_____

_____

_____

BY LAURA KRONSKE

SEWING AND QUILTING TIPS

BY LAURA KRONSKE

ART AND SCULPTURES I FELL IN LOVE WITH AND ART TIPS

_____

_____

_____

_____

_____

_____

_____

_____

_____

_____

_____

_____

_____

_____

_____

_____

_____

_____

_____

_____

BY LAURA KRONSKE

NEW DESIGNS FOR THE FUTURE

BY LAURA KRONSKE

ABOUT MY APOTHECARY

_____
_____
_____
_____
_____
_____
_____
_____
_____
_____
_____
_____
_____
_____
_____
_____
_____
_____
_____
_____

BY LAURA KRONSKE

HERBS AND PLANTS I LOVE

BY LAURA KRONSKE

FAVORITE TEAS AND RECIPES

_____

_____

_____

_____

_____

_____

_____

_____

_____

_____

_____

_____

_____

_____

_____

_____

_____

_____

_____

_____

BY LAURA KRONSKE

ALL ABOUT HOMEOPATHS THAT HAVE HELPED ME

BY LAURA KRONSKE

VITAMINS I ENJOY

_____

_____

_____

_____

_____

_____

_____

_____

_____

_____

_____

_____

_____

_____

_____

_____

_____

_____

BY LAURA KRONSKE

HYDROSOLS I USE

_____

_____

_____

_____

_____

_____

_____

_____

_____

_____

_____

_____

_____

_____

_____

_____

_____

_____

_____

_____

_____

By Laura Kronske

PHARMACEUTICALS I NEEDED AND WHY

_____

_____

_____

_____

_____

_____

_____

_____

_____

_____

_____

_____

_____

_____

_____

_____

_____

_____

_____

_____

_____

_____

By Laura Kronske

FUNNY JOKES AND STORIES I TOLD

BY LAURA KRONSKE

SAD STORIES I LEARNED FROM

_____
_____
_____
_____
_____
_____
_____
_____
_____
_____
_____
_____
_____
_____
_____
_____
_____
_____
_____

By Laura Kronske

STORIES WITH NO MEANING THAT I LOVED

BY LAURA KRONSKE

EMBARRASSING STORIES

BY LAURA KRONSKE

DESIGNATED ASSHOLES IN MY LIFE AND THE LESSON THEY TAUGHT ME

_____

_____

_____

_____

_____

_____

_____

_____

_____

_____

_____

_____

_____

_____

_____

_____

_____

By Laura Kronske

MY HAIR AND MAKE-UP STYLES AND TIPS

_____

_____

_____

_____

_____

_____

_____

_____

_____

_____

_____

_____

_____

_____

_____

_____

_____

_____

_____

_____

_____

BY LAURA KRONSKE

MY FAVORITE HIDING SPOTS

BY LAURA KRONSKE

MY FAVORITE HOT SPRINGS OR SWIMMING HOLE

_____

_____

_____

_____

_____

_____

_____

_____

_____

_____

_____

_____

_____

_____

_____

_____

_____

_____

_____

BY LAURA KRONSKE

WHY LIFE IS GOOD

_____

_____

_____

_____

_____

_____

_____

_____

_____

_____

_____

_____

_____

_____

_____

_____

_____

_____

_____

_____

_____

BY LAURA KRONSKE

WHY MY LIFE WAS AMAZING

_____

_____

_____

_____

_____

_____

_____

_____

_____

_____

_____

_____

_____

_____

_____

_____

_____

_____

_____

_____

By Laura Kronske

LESSONS I HAVE GATHERED FROM ALL OF MY EXPERIENCE

_____

_____

_____

_____

_____

_____

_____

_____

_____

_____

_____

_____

_____

_____

_____

_____

_____

_____

BY LAURA KRONSKE

"WHO IS BELOW WHAT'S ABOVE, AND
ABOVE WHAT'S BELOW?

-RIG VEDA

CHAPTER 12

🕇

"Know that the brightest blossoms are not always the tallest trees."

-The things trees know

Whether being bright or being tall is more important, it is up to you; maybe neither or both is important. Take a moment to express what was important to you. Death only signifies the end of a chapter. When we move on past this lifetime, we may have to return to earth to repeat lessons that need more attention, or we may ascend to the next dimension. Either way, our descendants will still be on earth mourning us and learning their own lessons from the way we lived our life. Use this information to express how you would like to be remembered. When death arrives our family, members are expected to plan our funeral, write our obituary, make important decisions about where the service will be held, where our final resting ground will be, and what to put it in at our funeral. They are expected to do this when they are fresh into an extreme state of mourning, sadness, and reflection. It is actually challenging to make those decisions in such a fragile and vulnerable state. Be specific when writing this chapter, as it will relieve many obstacles for your family upon your death. Time offers many opportunities but never second chances.

My death

OBITUARY

_____

_____

_____

_____

_____

_____

_____

_____

_____

_____

_____

_____

_____

_____

_____

_____

_____

_____

_____

By Laura Kronske

MY LIVING WILL AND LAST WISHES
(PLEASE BE ADVISED THAT SOME STATES AND COUNTRIES REQUIRE NOTARIZED WILLS)

_____

_____

_____

_____

_____

_____

_____

_____

_____

_____

_____

_____

_____

_____

_____

_____

_____

_____

_____

By Laura Kronske

MY REGULAR WILL LAST THOUGHTS

_____

_____

_____

_____

_____

_____

_____

_____

_____

_____

_____

_____

_____

_____

_____

_____

_____

_____

_____

_____

BY LAURA KRONSKE

MY EULOGY KEY POINTS

_____

_____

_____

_____

_____

_____

_____

_____

_____

_____

_____

_____

_____

_____

_____

_____

_____

_____

_____

_____

_____

_____

BY LAURA KRONSKE

MY FUNERAL IMPORTANT POINTS

_____

_____

_____

_____

_____

_____

_____

_____

_____

_____

_____

_____

_____

_____

_____

_____

_____

_____

_____

BY LAURA KRONSKE

MY BURIAL, SHOULD I BE BURIED OR CREMATED OR SOMETHING ENTIRELY DIFFERENT

_____

_____

_____

_____

_____

_____

_____

_____

_____

_____

_____

_____

_____

_____

_____

_____

_____

_____

By Laura Kronske

MY ESTATE INFO

_____

_____

_____

_____

_____

_____

_____

_____

_____

_____

_____

_____

_____

_____

_____

_____

_____

_____

_____

_____

By Laura Kronske

My contact numbers for stocks, bonds, insurance claims, safety deposit box keys, phone list for insurance claims, bank account info secret stashes, valuable items, vehicle titles and important forms

---

BY LAURA KRONSKE

WHAT OUTFIT TO BURY ME IN AND WHY?

_____

_____

_____

_____

_____

_____

_____

_____

_____

_____

_____

_____

_____

_____

_____

_____

_____

_____

_____

_____

By Laura Kronske

MY QUOTES, MEMORIES AND PICTURES TO REMEMBER ME BY TO MY FAMILY

BY LAURA KRONSKE

I'LL NEVER FORGET SECTION OF FAMILY MEMORIES AND MOMENTS OF JOY

_____

_____

_____

_____

_____

_____

_____

_____

_____

_____

_____

_____

_____

_____

_____

_____

_____

_____

_____

By Laura Kronske

MOMENTS THAT I APPRECIATE AND WANT TO SHARE WITH DESCENDANTS

_____

_____

_____

_____

_____

_____

_____

_____

_____

_____

_____

_____

_____

_____

_____

_____

_____

_____

_____

_____

BY LAURA KRONSKE

MY HOPE AND GOALS FOR THE FUTURE FOR ALL OF MY CHILDREN AND FAMILY

_____

_____

_____

_____

_____

_____

_____

_____

_____

_____

_____

_____

_____

_____

_____

_____

_____

BY LAURA KRONSKE

HOW I DIED. THE DATE, TIME, AND STORY

_____

_____

_____

_____

_____

_____

_____

_____

_____

_____

_____

_____

_____

_____

_____

_____

_____

_____

_____

_____

"It is not difficult to avoid death.
Gentlemen of the jury: it is much
more difficult to avoid wickedness,
for it runs faster than death"

-Socrates

By Laura Kronske

CHAPTER 13

🔱

"To find yourself, think for yourself."

-Socrates

Everyone in our lives holds a special place in our hearts in different amazing ways. Use this section to pass on the importance of everyone in your lives, moments they were there for you or inspired you. Ways they changed your lives and special memories. Tell them the stories they need to know and anything that might help them make it through life happy. I hope that my children can live in peace after I die, knowing that they are perfect, special and loved forever.

My Reflections

MY REFLECTIONS OF MYSELF

_____

_____

_____

_____

_____

_____

_____

_____

_____

_____

_____

_____

_____

_____

_____

_____

_____

_____

_____

_____

_____

_____

By Laura Kronske

MY LAST MESSAGE TO MY SPOUSE

_____

_____

_____

_____

_____

_____

_____

_____

_____

_____

_____

_____

_____

_____

_____

_____

_____

_____

_____

_____

_____

_____

By Laura Kronske

MY LAST MESSAGE TO MY PARENTS

_____

_____

_____

_____

_____

_____

_____

_____

_____

_____

_____

_____

_____

_____

_____

_____

_____

_____

_____

_____

By Laura Kronske

MY LAST MESSAGE TO MY CHILDREN

_____

_____

_____

_____

_____

_____

_____

_____

_____

_____

_____

_____

_____

_____

_____

_____

_____

_____

_____

_____

By Laura Kronske

MY LAST MESSAGE TO MY GRANDCHILDREN

_____

_____

_____

_____

_____

_____

_____

_____

_____

_____

_____

_____

_____

_____

_____

_____

_____

_____

_____

_____

_____

BY LAURA KRONSKE

MY LAST MESSAGE TO MY FAMILY

By Laura Kronske

MY LAST MESSAGE TO MY FRIENDS

_____

_____

_____

_____

_____

_____

_____

_____

_____

_____

_____

_____

_____

_____

_____

_____

_____

_____

_____

By Laura Kronske

MY LAST MESSAGE TO MY ACQUAINTANCES

_____

_____

_____

_____

_____

_____

_____

_____

_____

_____

_____

_____

_____

_____

_____

_____

_____

_____

_____

By Laura Kronske

"IF YOUR SHIP DOESN'T COME IN... SAIL INTO IT."

-JONATHAN WINTER

CHAPTER 14

"The steeper the mountain, the harder the climb, the better
the view from the finishing line."

Anonymous

So much grief and pain arise at the passing of a loved one. I
know this is not how I would wish my passing to be. Let us
rejoice in, and celebrate, the life of each other. Even though the
sorrow of losing each other is so strong right now, take a deep,
long, slow breath and smile. I will miss all of you so much, but
I will always be with you in spirit. Take this opportunity to
remember the good times, the stories you will pass on to your
children, and the unforgettable moments that will travel with
you in your heart. I only want your peace and happiness and
joy to shine today, tomorrow, and for eternity. I will see you
again when it is time. Love always....

My Family and friends last words to me.

MY FAMILY'S SIGNATURES AND LAST MESSAGES TO ME

_____

_____

_____

_____

_____

_____

_____

_____

_____

_____

_____

_____

_____

_____

_____

_____

_____

_____

BY LAURA KRONSKE

MY QUOTES, MEMORIES, AND PICTURES TO REMEMBER ME BY TO MY FAMILY

_____

_____

_____

_____

_____

_____

_____

_____

_____

_____

_____

_____

_____

_____

_____

_____

_____

_____

_____

BY LAURA KRONSKE

ALL OF THE BEAUTIFUL PICTURES OF MY LIFE

_____

_____

_____

_____

_____

_____

_____

_____

_____

_____

_____

_____

_____

_____

_____

_____

_____

_____

BY LAURA KRONSKE

"THINGS WORK OUT THE BEST FOR
PEOPLE WHO MAKE THE BEST OF THINGS"

- JOHN WOODEN

www.ingramcontent.com/pod-product-compliance
Lightning Source LLC
Chambersburg PA
CBHW021351090426
42742CB00009B/810